Saving Pocket

by

Elizabeth Bernays

and

Linda Gheen

This is the true story of a desert cottontail rabbit found as a newborn on the blacktopped road in Tucson, Arizona, in March 2007. Dr. Anna in the story is the book's author. Sam in the story is the photographer. The book was published in August 2007.

ISBN 978-1-60461-024-6

Saving Pocket

It was a warm sunny morning in March when Sam and Dr. Anna took Bailey the Labrador for a walk. Turning a corner they saw a tiny dark mouse-like thing on the burning blacktopped road.

Bailey ran up to it followed by Sam. It was a helpless newborn rabbit whose mother had been killed by a car. Its eyes were closed and it had just a few black hairs on its back.

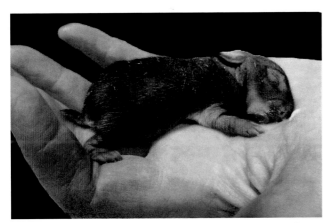

Dr. Anna picked it up and was happy when she saw movement, but it was not strong enough to stand up.

"Can we keep it?" asked Sam.

"Not unless we can find out how to care for it properly," replied Dr. Anna.

They went home to check on the Internet how to raise wild cottontail bunnies. There was plenty of advice but they also found out that only one or two out of a hundred baby bunnies survive when people try to keep them.

Sam said, "*Please* - you could be its mommy."

Sam put the tiny bunny in her shirt pocket and they went to the store to buy kitten formula and human baby vitamins. Sam stroked its smooth little head with her finger and decided that the bunny must be a little girl and her name would be "Pocket."

They made the milky food and Dr. Anna dripped it into Pocket's mouth with a dropper, but most of it dribbled out. Would they be able to make the little bunny eat?

Dr. Anna wiped the bunny's little chin, and then its back end with a warm wet cloth, hoping it would feel like a mother's tongue. The mother does this to make the very young bunnies relieve themselves, and also to keep them clean.

At first nothing happened and Dr. Anna was worried. Sam said, "She has to do *something*." At the first sign of yellow liquid and tiny pellets like black pinheads after her third small feed, Dr. Anna said, "Oh, this is progress!" And they laughed because they were both so happy.

The little bunny learned to eat from the dropper and Dr.

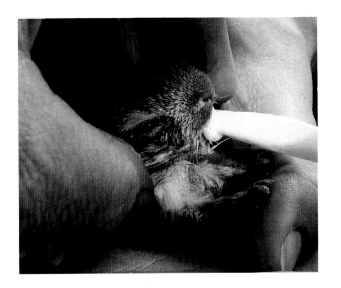

Anna fed her every few hours. When Pocket sensed the food at the tip of the dropper, she opened her mouth and started sucking. When she had enough she let the formula dribble down her chin.

Pocket snuggled into the corners of her box and when Sam and Dr. Anna visited friends they carried her in their pockets, taking formula with them.

When Pocket was a week old she opened her eyes, but they were still quite small. Her ears had grown a lot bigger and her hair had become fluffy. She looked much more like a bunny and she peed and made lots of pellets all by herself.

But Pocket was still very small.

Sam put her on the ground outside and allowed her to have her first experience in the natural world. There, on the dead leaves and rough stones she took her first few wobbly steps, but Sam soon put her back in her box for safety.

Already her little tail had started to grow white and fluffy.

Dr. Anna continued to give her lots of formula just after she got up in the morning and when she went to bed. They were so happy at how well their little adopted desert cottontail bunny was doing.

Pocket's ears got longer and her eyes got bigger. Her fluffy coat got shaggy. She was growing well. Each day Sam let her test the desert environment. She seemed most comfortable in protected corners, in pockets, or in their curled hands.

She even seemed happy just crawling on a lap or up a shirtfront. When Sam or Dr. Anna took her out to hold her and feed her she became very quiet and relaxed when they stroked her along her back, and she never tried to run away.

Pocket became quite used to being handled by both Sam and Dr. Anna and showed no sign of being afraid.

Each day she ate more of the formula and she began to suck it so well that hardly any of it was wasted. Just a few drops dribbled down her front and she even started to clean herself after her chin had been wiped with paper towel, her tiny tongue working from side to side.

As Pocket grew more active, the cardboard box became a bit cramped, so Sam got a small dog crate for her. She put in a T-shirt for

a nest as well as some dry grass and other leaves so the bunny had a bigger home. Pretty soon Pocket was running around in the crate and sleeping in the nest. Sam gave her a clean T-shirt every couple of days but mostly she peed and left her droppings on the leaves, and kept her nest area clean.

When Pocket was nearly three weeks old she got her first solid food. Dr. Anna and Sam gave her all kinds of different things such as flowers, wheat bread, alfalfa sprouts, spinach, carrots and kale. They wanted to make sure she

had a good choice and that the food was nutritious. They also gave her a bowl of water, though in nature the desert cottontails often have to rely on getting water in their food.

When they saw her eat a little of each food and stand up on her back legs at the water bowl they felt they could relax.

During Pocket's fourth week, while she was getting both formula and solid food she started scratching herself. First she scratched her face and chin and then her chest.

Fur started falling out. The gingery-colored hair on the back of her neck got thin and soon her

cheeks were bare and her neck and chest lost most of the fur. Dr. Anna was worried.

It was back to the Internet. They discovered that weaning was a difficult time. Rabbits need special bacteria in their digestive systems to help digest leaves and grain. In nature the young bunnies get the bacteria by eating their mothers' droppings. So what's next? Pocket had no mother!

They transferred Pocket to Bailey the Labrador's big crate and gathered desert soil and leaves. Then Dr. Anna found fresh droppings in the desert and put them in Pocket's water, so when she had a drink she could get the bacteria with her water. Happily, Pocket drank the dirty water!

Soon Pocket was growing new, soft fur and getting very active, and she almost filled Dr. Anna's hand.

They gave her vegetables and native desert plants, as she needed to learn to eat her natural foods if she was ever to be a successful free bunny. Pocket's favorite foods were cilantro, kale and mesquite leaves. She also liked grass, desert plants and flowers. As she got bigger she ate mesquite seedpods, and tried just a little bit of different strong-smelling plants that are found growing in the desert.

Pocket grew well. Her eyes became big and bright, her ears longer than ever, and her cottontail very fluffy. She groomed herself and spent a lot of time twitching her nose.

When Sam took food to her and called "Pocket," she ran to the door of the crate. Sometimes she jumped on top of her nest box to look out, or stood up on her back legs, or ran in circles then rolled wildly in the leaf litter, giving the two human mommies a warm fuzzy feeling themselves.

Sam and Dr. Anna measured Pocket's growth on kitchen scales. At first she had been too small to register a weight, but at seven weeks, she weighed eight ounces, about a fifth of normal adult weight for a cottontail rabbit.

Her ears and eyes and feet became so big compared with the rest of her, but she would need those huge ears to help lose heat in the hot summer, the big bulging eyes to see and escape from danger, and big feet to jump and kick.

In nature, desert cottontails must be alert for so many different predators. There are eagles, hawks, owls, snakes, coyotes and bobcats in the Arizona deserts. And always there are the dangers of humans and their cars. So far, Pocket just had short, supervised visits to the desert outside where she sniffed all the desert plants.

When Pocket was two months old Dr. Anna and Sam put her big crate out into a courtyard among the trees and shrubs. She needed to get used to life under more natural conditions. She would have to get used to hot days and cool nights, trees blowing in the wind, and the sight and sound of all the birds.

From the window Dr. Anna and Sam, Yoyo the calico cat and Bailey the Labrador, could all watch the antics of the little bunny, and each morning Dr. Anna was there to look out and make sure she was all right.

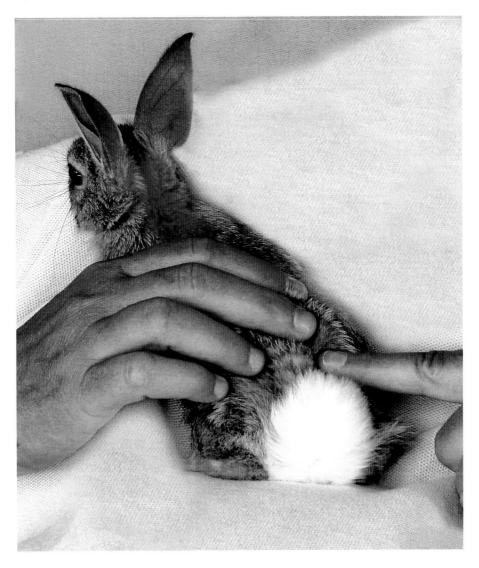

Pocket's neck was rust colored and her tail white and fluffy.

Pocket was lively in her cage outside yet quiet and calm when she was held. Dr. Anna and Sam were happy to have raised her successfully so far.

"Can't we keep her?" Asked Sam.

"We have to let her go."

Dr. Anna also said that it wouldn't be right to keep a wild animal in a cage.

So Sam became fonder of Pocket, and spent more time with her.

Pocket was becoming a fine young cottontail. Dr. Anna and Sam saw how much she had grown and felt it was time to think about the best way to free her. They decided on a "soft release." This would mean doing it in stages, first being released into an enclosed courtyard and later being allowed to go completely free.

They made sure the shady green courtyard was enclosed with wire netting. They would open the cage door when she was ten weeks old. Then the last day came. They looked out the window. Pocket was on top of her nest box, looking out as quail scratched in the dirt nearby and hummingbirds came to the feeder above. She still had a pile of mesquite leaves and carrot tops to eat. The courtyard was cool and shady with lots of hiding places. At least she had a good start in life, they thought as they looked at bright-eyed Pocket.

Dr. Anna and Sam were both a little sad wondering if she would be able to manage on her own, but they were also excited to think their bunny would soon be free.

They each said goodbye to Pocket in their own way then put her back in the cage for her last hours of feeding in captivity. At last, Sam opened the door and they sat nearby to watch.

Pocket didn't notice the open door, but suddenly, after about half an hour, she was at the cage door jumping out. When she was first out she was a bit wary, but then she went wild. She ran and ran, all over the courtyard, jumping up in the air and kicking wildly. It was such a fantastic sight - she seemed so happy to be free and to have so much room to run.

Dr. Anna said they should leave lots of food in the crate so she could always go back in when she was hungry, but they only saw quail in the cage.

Few of the plants growing in the courtyard were good for Pocket, so each day Dr. Anna and Sam put food out beside a water bowl, calling "Pocket" and she often came. She explored the area but had favorite hiding places and dug small depressions in the dirt to rest in.

The big day was to come when she would be allowed complete freedom. She would face the world of other bunnies outside the courtyard, as well as all the predators. She would have to learn to find her own shelter, food and water.

Pocket was three months old on a day in June when Sam opened the gate. In five minutes Pocket was gone. They were sad and happy at the same time.

They had raised a healthy desert cottontail rabbit and allowed her to join the natural world.

Sometimes they saw a young bunny with a rusty colored neck hopping outside the window, scratching itself, or resting under a bush, and wondered if it was Pocket.

A week after her release, in the heat of the summer when food was scarce, a small bunny came into the courtyard. She came to the call of "Pocket" and ate the cilantro she was offered. What a thrill it was that she knew where to come in the tough heat of June.

As the days got hotter, up to 110^{0}F, and the desert even drier than usual, Sam thought it would be helpful to keep her again in the courtyard. So one day, when Pocket was inside eating corn, Sam closed the gate to keep her in.

But Pocket had other ideas. She already knew freedom and soon discovered she could now jump over the wall. And jump she did.

So Sam and Dr. Anna left the gate open for Pocket to come and go easily. Sometimes they saw her nibbling at dead leaves or the few native plants in the courtyard, just as other bunnies did.

Each day they took some carrots, corn or cilantro to the place by the water bowl and called for Pocket. Often she came, or if she didn't come right away they would

see her feeding there later. Some days there was no sign of Pocket.

Sam could tell which was Pocket if a group of bunnies were in the courtyard, because when she went out with food the others ran off and Pocket stayed behind.

At intervals during that hot summer, Pocket came back. She was the lucky bunny that got food supplements when the desert was brown and barren.

Dr. Anna and Sam felt they too had been the lucky ones to have the joy of saving Pocket and keeping her for a while.

****

Somewhere out there Pocket will have found a mate and had her own babies. Somewhere out there Pocket's family is living as desert bunnies should – wild and free.

The Tale of a Tail

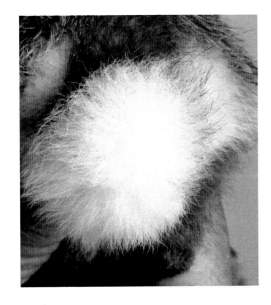